SOUTHERN ITALY

A Travel Guide Book for Visiting Puglia, Tasting Delicious Food

and Have an Amazing Tour Among the Best Places of This Enchanted Land.

Written By

Domenico Cirone

Contents

Want help planning your vacation in Puglia?

Scan This QR to Discover Free Tips for Traveling in Puglia, Visiting its Enchanting Places and Eating Delicious Food!

CHAPTER 1

10 FEATURES OF PUGLIA YOU NEED TO KNOW ABOUT

Apulia is a region in southern Italy bordering Molise to the northwest, Campania and Basilicata to the west, the Adriatic Sea to the east and north, and the Ionian Sea to the south.

The provincial capital is Bari and the other provinces are Brindisi, Foggia, Lecce, Taranto and Barletta-Andria-Trani, the latter established in 2008.

The combination of attractions that this land holds, from the 860 kilometres of coastline with sheer cliffs and Caribbean beaches, to quality food and wine, is truly delightful: Altamura DOP bread, capocollo di Martina Franca, bombette di Cisternino, extra virgin olive oils and Primitivo, Negroamaro and Nero di Troia wines are just some of the regional excellences. Rupestrian churches, Romanesque cathedrals, the castles of Frederick II and Baroque treasures enrich its artistic profile.

Apulia is the trulli, ravines, puli and dolinas, the Gargano and Murge National Parks, the marine reserves of the Tremiti Islands and Torre Guaceto. Apulia is the basilicas, cathedrals and sanctuaries, different artistic expressions united by faith; it is the famous terracotta whistles of Rutigliano, the lace of the Gargano, the ceramic products of Grottaglie, and the artefacts made in Salento from the tender Lecce stone, wrought iron and papier-mâché. Apulia is the rhythms and colours of the Taranta and the Salento Pizzica, which receive due homage in the famous Notte della Taranta, which has now become the largest festival in Italy dedicated to this traditional dance with ancestral anthropological overtones and one of the most significant events on popular culture in Europe.

Puglia is a spectacular land, a bridge between West and East, a land of smells, colours, flavours and poetry. This region is the birthplace of such personalities as Aldo Moro, Rodolfo Valentino, Lino Banfi, Checco Zalone, Pietro Mennea and many others. There are many reasons to visit Puglia, the easternmost part of the boot, but these 10 are sure to be enough to organise a visit right away.

1. THE SEA

The Apulian Sea has a thousand shades of blue and azure. With 800 km of coastline, many of them beautiful beaches, among the best in the Adriatic and in Italy, Apulia is the region of the sea, uncontaminated waters to be seen, smelled and explored.

Faraglioni di Torre Sant'Andrea, Melendugno, OT, Puglia, Italy

2. THE FOOD

Here you can eat well and eat a lot, Apulia is a region of genuine cuisine and ancient flavours. There are many dishes and specialities to try, each one better than the last, so be prepared to leave with a few extra kilos. Taralli, burrata, fragrant bread, orecchiette with turnip tops, caciocavallo, cartellate, the best oil in the world... Are you already salivating?

In addition to what has already been listed, the Apulians also have an eye for traditional breeding and for fish caught every night, therefore always very fresh.

Focaccia pugliese

3. THE PEOPLE

When visiting Apulia, you will immediately notice the warmth of the people. Apulians are definitely friendly and finding smiles and a warm welcome, I think, is an important factor in choosing your next destination.

Tourists from all over the world talk about how the people of Puglia made them feel at home from the start, forever carrying the memory of a beautiful vacation in their hearts.

Southern people in particular have always been accustomed to welcoming guests into their homes, so it is very easy to make connections with locals, who will not hesitate to help you if you get lost in the streets of the cities you will visit.

An old Apulian man wearing a Coppola, a common hat in Puglia.

4. THE TRULLI

Trulli are unique, dry-stone constructions, a Unesco heritage site. Mostly you can find them in Alberobello, but the whole area is dotted with them.

Trulli have this particular shape because they were made in ancient times without the use of adhesives, taking advantage only of their wedge-shaped construction.

They have the particularity of maintaining pleasantly cool temperatures during the summer and temperate during the winter, as the stone they are made of insulates the interior from the outside temperature.

The construction of these houses is only possible because of the predominantly karst terrain of Puglia, which has expanses of land called "Murgia," rich in rocks that are used in the construction of these houses and the famous dry stone walls.

Alberobello

5. THE LANDSCAPES

Not only the blue of the sea and sky, merging on the horizon, but also the white stones, the red earth and the green of nature. Apulia is a harmonious palette of colours and a union of different landscapes: the sea, the mountains of the Subappennines and the boundless plains.

Polignano a Mare

6. THE BAROQUE

Between the 16th and 17th centuries, this artistic and architectural current developed, the Apulian Baroque, which you can find and admire especially in Lecce, Galatina, Nardò or Gallipoli. What characterises it is certainly the sumptuousness of the decorative elements on both secular and religious buildings.

Basilica of Holy Cross

7. MUSIC

Especially if you are in Apulia in summer, you cannot fail to immerse your-self in the music of this region. In the squares of many towns, there are festivals and concerts, sometimes even free of charge. And then there is the pizzica, or taranta. The music of Salento, a music to be danced to, as if a tarantula had plucked you, a music linked to the cult of Dionysus, a music with an ancient flavour, linked to the territory.

Melpignano hosts the big summer concert, the Notte della Taranta, in August, where almost 200,000 people dance until dawn in the streets and squares.

Taranta Night

8. TRADITIONS

Some traditions, such as the pizzica, the trulli, the production of Altamura bread, we have already mentioned. But there are many others, such as eating raw fish with your feet in the sand or winter and summer carnivals, which I will leave unmentioned here. Immerse yourself in this land and savour them all.

One of the Putignano's carnival floats

9. HISTORY

Traditionally, because of its location, Apulia has been somewhat of a bridge between two worlds, being influenced by the western Roman-Germanic culture, but also by the more eastern Greek-Byzantine one. In culture and art, the passage through this land of different peoples is clear: the Romans, Byzantines, Normans, Aragonese and Bourbons.

10. OSTUNI

But also, Locorotondo or Polignano a mare, little white towns overlooking the Adriatic Sea and surrounded by fragrant olive trees. Ostuni, the White City, is just one of the villages to be discovered when visiting and getting to know Apulia, with its countless narrow streets, steps and white walls highlighted by colourful flowers on the window sills.

Ostuni

CHAPTER 2

APULIAN FOOD TO BE ABSOLUTELY TASTED

Apulia is a land rich in beauty, colours and flavours, and its food and wine also respects the traits of this region of our peninsula. The typical Apulian dishes are numerous and fall perfectly within the Mediterranean tradition.

Among both first courses, main courses and desserts, there are specialities that are not only known locally but exported worldwide. Here is a list of typical Apulian dishes.

TYPICAL APULIAN DISHES: FIRST COURSES

As is the case for all Italian cuisine, the first courses of Apulian cuisine represent a highlight of this food and wine tradition.

1. ORECCHIETTE WITH TURNIP TOPS

This is par excellence the most renowned of Puglia's typical foods, at least among those known outside the region. Orecchiette is a pasta that is prepared by hand using small concave disks, obtained by pressing with the thumb.

Its seasoning with turnip tops, to which anchovies, oil and garlic are added, is a local speciality, the result of the abundance of particular vegetables.

Orecchiette pasta with turnip tops

2. CALZONE BARESE

The calzone barese, as its name suggests, originates from the city of Bari. In fact, in the local tradition, the calzone is a timbale of dough that is made by hand and then filled with a number of very delicious ingredients.

One is ricotta, which is, however, a very different cheese from the classic ricotta: in fact, it has a creamy consistency and is rather spicy. In addition to this ingredient, olives, anchovies, sultanas and fried onions are added.

Calzone with turnip tops

3. RICE TIELLA

Tiella di riso is a kind of local paella whose name derives from the container in which it is cooked, namely an earthenware pot. It is made with rice, potatoes and mussels, to which other ingredients are added, making it very delicious. These are tomatoes, onion, breadcrumbs, parsley and garlic.

Rice, potatoes and mussels

4. FRIED PANZEROTTI

The fried panzerotto is another popular local speciality. It is a particularly pleasant street food: it is a kind of calzone, crescent-shaped, made of pizza dough filled with mozzarella and tomato. It is then fried so that it remains crispy on the outside and soft on the inside.

Panzerotto

APULIAN MAIN COURSES

Apulia is not only the land of first courses. Traditional Apulian dishes also rightly include main courses, with meat, fish and vegetable dishes.

1. FRIED LAMPASCIONI

Lampascioni are typical products of this region and have recently received official recognition as traditional Italian products. They are spring onions that grow wild and are found, in particular, in the Murgia and Bari areas.

Their organoleptic characteristics make them very special as they have a sweet and aromatic smell but at the same time note a slightly bitter aftertaste.

Fried lampascioni are a simple dish, but at the same time particularly tasty, as they represent well the essence of the region where they are produced.

Fired Lampascioni

2. OCTOPUS ALLA PIGNATA

Octopus alla pignata is another typical dish of this area. Octopuses, which are particularly delicious in the waters of Apulia, are cooked in their own water.

The name pignata is another term for the tiella, that terracotta pot used to prepare many dishes. In this pot, the octopus is cooked for a long time so that the meat is perfectly tender and tasty.

Octopus alla Pignata

3. MEAT ROLLS: THE MARRO (INVOLTINI, "GNUMREDD")

If Apulia is a region famous for its vegetables, meat also best represents the character of the Apulian hinterland. The dish made from lamb roulades, for which the innards are used, is called marro.

These are treated in a special way to create a roulade with their skin and are stuffed with particularly fine ingredients such as pecorino cheese, parsley and garlic, which bring out the best flavour of the lamb.

Gnumredd

4. BRACIOLE

Brasciole are another typical meat dish of this region. In the original recipe, they are formed into rolls with horse meat, as is the tradition in Bari.

Today, however, they are often replaced by beef. They are prepared with gravy and give a delicious and delicate flavour.

Braciole

APULIAN DAIRY PRODUCTS

The entire region of Puglia is dotted with a myriad of farms where you can find Apulian dairy products and cheeses.Over time, fathers have passed down to their sons the knowledge related to animal husbandry and cheese production.

The most substantial part of Apulian dairy production comes from sheep's milk: even today, driving along the roads of this long region, it is not difficult to come across flocks of grazing sheep or real transhumance.

- Several delicious products are made from sheep's milk: ricotta, primo sale, giuncata (also often offered flavored with rucola, walnuts or spices), ricotta salata, ricotta forte, and caciotta.
- Excellent mozzarella, nodini, braids, stuffed rolls, stracciatelle, burrate and scamorze are created from cow's milk.
- From the milk of podolica cows, which is fatter, caciocavallo cheese is made.

There are several dairy products produced in Puglia, such as burrata, caciocavallo, scamorza, stracciatella, ricotta, ricotta forte and many other wonderful products all to be tasted...

Apulian Burrata

TYPICAL APULIAN SWEETS

In the list of typical Apulian dishes, sweets are certainly not missing. Here are two in particular:

1. PASTICCIOTTO

Pasticciotto is a very old typical sweet, at least that is how it is said, and is one of the most famous of Italian pastries. According to tradition, it dates back to the late 18th century when a cook, no longer having enough dough to make a cake, created smaller pastries.

They are, in fact, oval-shaped cakes with an outer pastry dough and a custard filling. It is a mouth-watering dessert perfect for any time of day.

Pasticciotto from Lecce

2. CARTELLATE

Among the local desserts, we cannot fail to mention cartellate, or carted-date, as they are called in the local dialect. These are puff pastry fritters enriched with honey and spices, vincotto and almonds. It is customary to eat them on various feast days but also at Christmas time.

Apulian Cartellate

CHAPTER 3

APULIAN BEACHES NOT TO BE MISSED

We really do have it all in Italy, from the Alps and the Dolomites in northern Italy, to the beautiful hills of Tuscany, through the famous cities of art, to the incredible beaches with white sand and crystal-clear water.

Baia dei Turchi, Otranto, Salento, Puglia, Italia

And on this last point, Puglia has nothing to envy anyone, with some of the most beautiful beaches in the country, such as the Maldives of Salento. But not only that, this aspect is mixed with culture, good food and the many cities that this region, known as "Italy's gateway to the East," has to offer. Let's see together then what are the 10 most beautiful beaches in Puglia.

MALDIVE OF SALENTO, MARINA OF PESCOLUSE

One of the most beautiful beaches in Puglia and Italy. We are talking about the Maldives of Salento, in Marina di Pescoluse, in the heel of the boot. Over the years it has received numerous awards and recognitions and is perfect for both families and young people. The establishment, open daily from 7 a.m. to 10 p.m., has everything you need for a perfect day of relaxation at the beach: umbrellas, deckchairs and sunbeds, a well-stocked newsstand, a bar and two lunchtime venues, and several stores selling beach items and souvenirs.

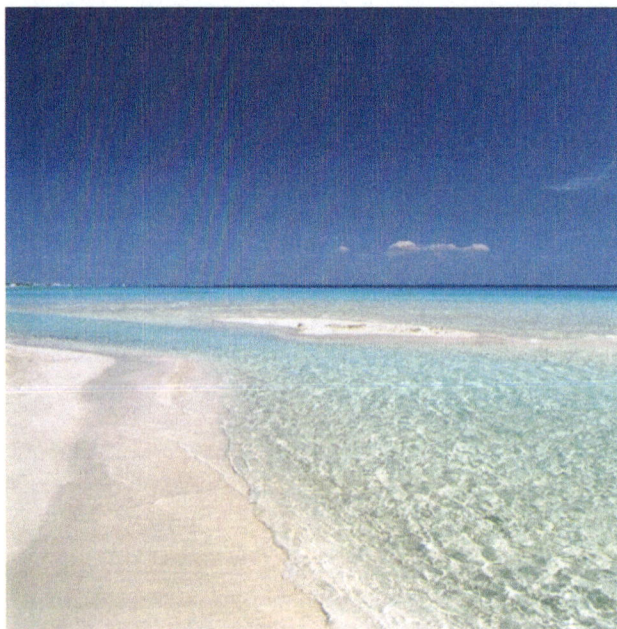

Maldive of Salento

For the sportier, you'll find beach volleyball courts, a pedal boat and jet ski rental service, and an extensive program with free pizzica, aerobics and zumba classes. Also available by reservation is a private area for relaxing away from the hustle and bustle. All this surrounded by a wonderfully blue sea, which has absolutely nothing to envy the Maldives. (For real.)

It is 2.5 kilometers from the center of Marina, a 30-minute walk; 78 kilometers from Lecce, about an hour by car, which can also be reached by bus 108 "City Terminal, getting off at the "Bar del Corso / Tabacchi" stop in the center of Marina di Pescoluse.

PUNTA PROSCIUTTO

Punta Prosciutto beach is located on the border between the provinces of Taranto and Lecce and is part of the Palude del Conte and Duna Costiera Natural Park, nestled between Torre Colimena to the north and Torre Lapillo to the south. This dreamy shoreline, with crystal-clear water and white sand, perfect for children to play, is mostly free, you will in fact be faced with a long, unspoiled beach.

If you prefer beach establishments don't worry, Punta Prosciutto also has some areas with umbrellas, sunbeds and deck chairs. In addition, the beach is popular with lovers of water sports, such as windsurfing, sailing, and diving.

The beach is only 300 meters from the center of Punta Prosciutto, about a 5-minute walk; 45 kilometers from Lecce, about 40 min by car.

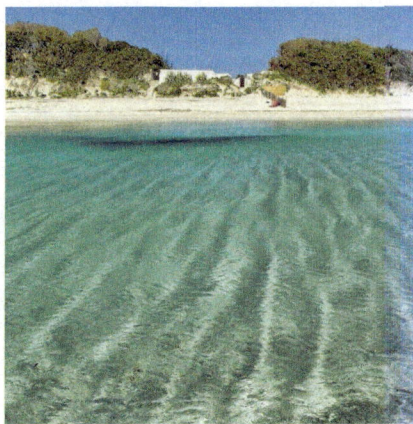

Punta Prosciutto

BAY OF TURKS

The Baia dei Turchi is located between Otranto and Torre dell'Orso, another beautiful beach further north. Included in the protected oasis of Laghi Alimini, it proudly sports the blue flag as a sign of its quality.

Bay of Turks

The white sandy beach is nestled between rock and pine forest. There are two ways to reach it: either by walking through the dense pine forest and dunes until you reach the beach, or by taking one of the shuttle buses that in warm weather take bathers from the parking lots to their destination.

The lido is mainly occupied by umbrellas and sunbeds and a few bars selling cold drinks and sandwiches, but nearby it is full of smaller, quieter and more secluded coves in which to seek more relaxation. But this area is also an important historical place: this is the spot where, back in 1480, the Saracens landed on their way to conquer Otranto. From this event came the name "Bay of the Turks."

It is located 7 km from Otranto (14 min by car) and 50 km from Lecce (about 45 min by car).

TOWER POZZELLE, OSTUNI

Torre Pozzelle beach is located a few kilometers from Ostuni and Brindisi. The best way to reach it is by car, as there are no bus connections to the city centers. This is one of the most beautiful and unspoiled beaches in Ostuni and does not correspond to a single beach, but consists of as many as 5 different small sandy coves.

From the parking lot you can access the first cove, the highest one, where guests of the nearby "Torre Pozzelle Camping" also often stop and where you can also find two clubs perfect for a cool drink or a lunch break sheltered from the sun. If you are looking for more tranquility, we recommend walking along the coast until you reach the other coves. Everywhere you will find free beaches and beautiful crystalline sea. Here, nature and the sea are the undisputed masters of the area.

It is 12 km from Ostuni, 17 minutes by car; 35 km from Brindisi, about 30 minutes by car; not accessible by public transportation.

Tower Pozzelle

LONG COVE, PESCHICI

Cala Lunga beach is located a few kilometers from Peschici and close to the Gargano National Park, a protected area of more than 120,000 square kilometers, rich in forests and archipelagos, in northern Apulia. In this bay, nestled between two rocky ridges, you will find soft, golden sand and from a beautiful crystal-clear sea with an always sandy bottom.

Long Cove

To reach it, you will have to follow the path from the free parking lot down to the beach, occupied by umbrellas and sunbeds, with bar service. From here you can also do some walking, for example you can follow the path that will take you to the Calalunga Tower, from which you can enjoy a breathtaking view. It is undoubtedly among the best beaches in Peschici.

It is located in Contrada Calalunga, Peschici, in the province of Foggia; 8 km from Peschici, 17 minutes by car; 18 km from Vieste, 28 minutes by car; 110 km from Foggia, almost 2 hours by car; not accessible by public transportation.

AQUAVIVA COVE, MARITIME MARINA

Acquaviva Cove is located in Marina di Marittima, a seaside resort in the province of Lecce.

Here you will be able to see a small fjord without having to go all the way to Norway. This, in fact, is a different beach from the others presented so far. First of all, it is a small bay composed of rocks and pebbles that creeps between the rocks and among the vegetation for about ten meters. Its name comes from the cold-water springs not far away. And, even here, the water is always colder than at other beaches. Also, since it is a free beach with no establishments, it is very quiet and sheltered.

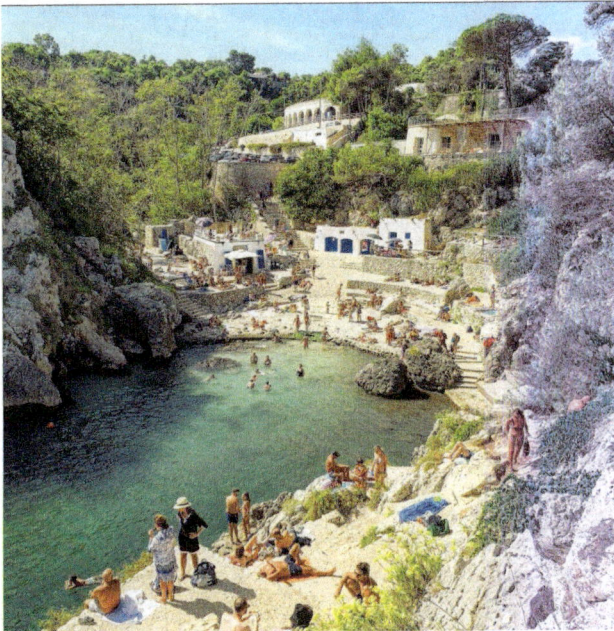

Acquaviva Cove

It is 600 meters from the center of Marina di Marittima, about 7 min on foot; 2 km from the center of Marittima, about half an hour on foot or 5 min by car; 50 km from Lecce, about 45 min by car, which can also be reached by bus 106 to Otranto, and from there take then bus 105 to the "Insenatura Acquaviva" stop in Marina di Marittima.

PUNTA DELLA SUINA, GALLIPOLI

Punta della Suina is a beach located in Gallipoli, on the coast of the Regional Natural Park Isola di Sant'Andrea e Litorale di Punta Pizzo. Its beautiful crystal clear water and white sand have earned it the name "Caribbean of the Ionian Sea." The beach is easily accessible through the pine forest and is equipped with umbrellas, sunbeds and deckchairs, and there is also a pedal boat service available to tourists. On the terrace-bar you can have a cool drink or enjoy a relaxing lunch break while admiring the beautiful view of the Bay of Gallipoli, all accompanied by background music.

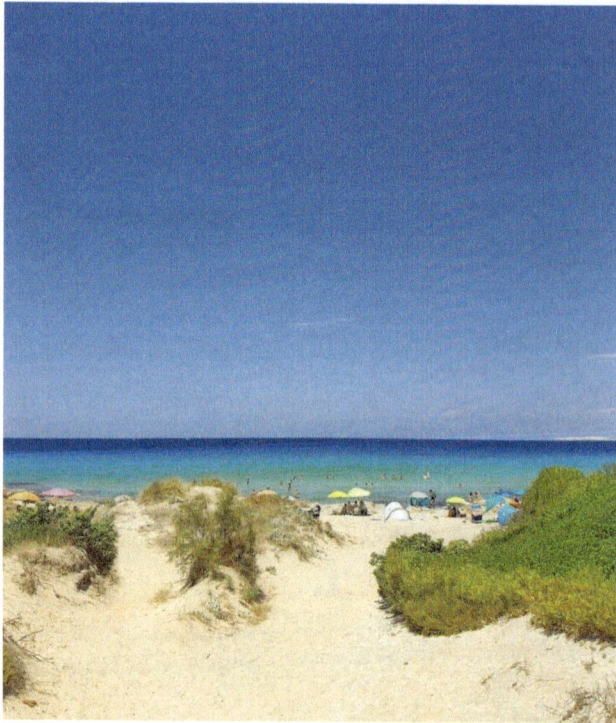

Punta della Suina

It is located on the coast of the Regional Natural Park Isola di Sant'Andrea e Litorale di Punta Pizzo, in the province of Lecce; only 9.4 km from Gallipoli, about 20 min by car; starting from Lecce there is a Pullman service to "Baia di Gallipoli - lido Punta della Suina".

BAY OF ZAGARE, MATTINATA

Bay of Zagare, also known as Baia dei Mergoli, is a stretch of coastline near Mattinata, Gargano, in the northern part of Puglia. Its name comes from zagare, or a citrus flower, of which the area is full.

This is one of the symbolic beaches of the entire Gargano, thanks to its high white cliffs and the presence of two limestone stacks, sculpted over the century by wind and other weathering.

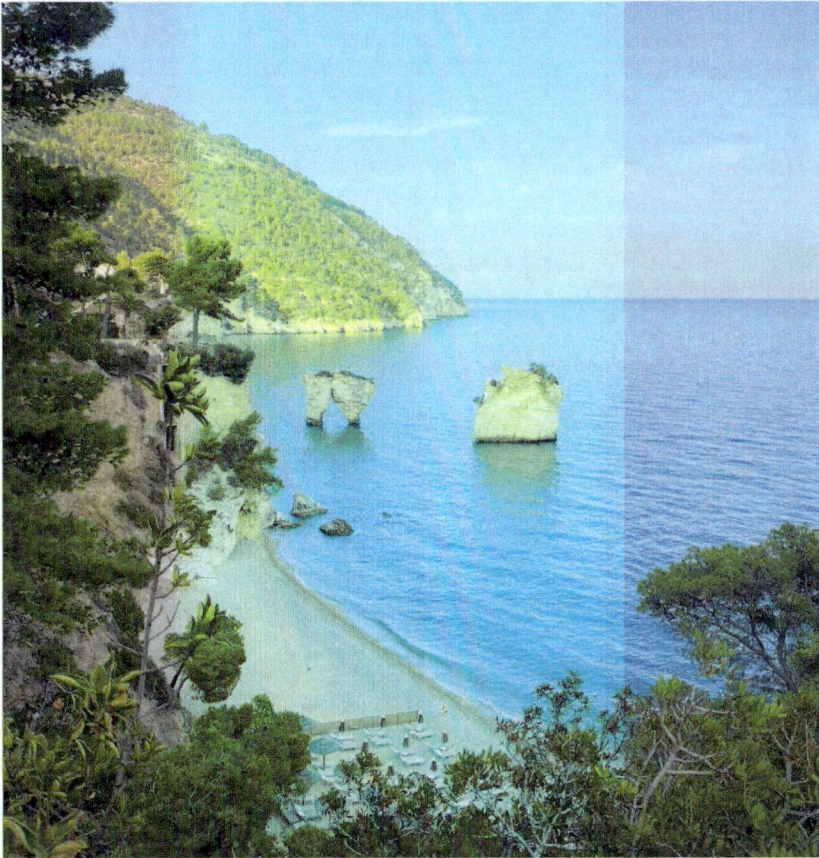

Bay of Zagre

Between the cliffs are several small coves, and this is the perfect area to organize a boat trip, exploring the area and the sea caves of the Gargano and seeing the stacks more closely. The area is made even more beautiful by the magnificent contrast between the crystal-clear water of the sea and the white cliffs.

It is 13 km from Mattinata, 14 min by car; 28 km from Manfredonia, about 30 min by car; 67 km from Foggia, almost an hour by car; not accessible by public transportation.

BAY OF MANACCORA

Manaccora Bay, also made famous by the cave of the same name. It is located close to the Gargano National Park, on the same shoreline as Cala Lunga Bay, from which it is about 2 kilometers, 5 minutes by car, and to which it is connected by a beaten path that can be walked in about 15 to 20 minutes. This beach, set between two rocky headlands and lots of greenery, is one of the most popular in the area.

Bay of Manaccora

Characterized by soft golden sand, most of it is occupied by the bathing establishment with umbrellas and sunbeds, another part is reserved for the tourist village and camping, and a small area is free. You can find several clubs and restaurants, which come alive in the evening by getting the party started. Walking along the shoreline, on the other hand, you can get to the

Manaccora Cave, a natural cave where signs of human settlement during the Bronze Age have been found.

It is 7.7 km from Peschici, 15 min by car; 23 km from Vieste, 33 min by car; 118 km from Foggia, almost 2 hours by car; not accessible by public transportation.

LAMA MONACHILE, POLIGNANO A MARE

Lama Monachile is perhaps one of the most famous beaches in Puglia because of its location: in fact, it is located in Polignano a Mare, a town loved by all, a romantic and charming destination. Reaching the bay is very easy, in fact it is located on the outskirts of the city, just 600 meters from the center. It is located on the bed of a very ancient stream now dried up, which flowed directly into the Mediterranean.

Since it is a small beach, easily accessible and located between the houses of the city, we recommend that you go early in the morning so that you can experience it in peace. To reach it, you can use the stairs that descend quickly from the adjacent bridge. Absolutely recommended for a visit or for a relaxing afternoon or morning, admiring the sea on one side and the beautiful Polignano a Mare on the other. If you want to admire the beach from a different perspective, we recommend a nice boat tour including an aperitif, you will have a cool and unforgettable experience.

It is located on Via S. Vito, in Polignano a Mare, 600 meters from the center of Marina, 8 minutes on foot; 34 km from Bari, 35 min by car, also reachable by regional train that connects Bari to Polignano a Mare in 45 minutes; 50 km from Ostuni, 45 min by car, also reachable by direct bus to Polignano.

Lama Monachile

CHAPTER 4

NATURAL AREAS TO VISIT IN APULIA

GARGANO NATIONAL PARK

Covering an area of more than 120,000 hectares, the Gargano National Park is all about discovering ancient forests and archipelagos bathed in crystal clear water.

Almost a region within a region, the Gargano National Park covers an area of more than 120,000 hectares hosting countless habitats.

Several protected areas are located here, including the Tremiti Islands Marine Reserve, unique for the extraordinary beauty of its seabed and natural caves.

In the hinterland of the Gargano promontory greens the last vestige of the Foresta Umbra, an extensive habitat even in prehistoric times.

There are many opportunities to explore the park on foot or by bicycle thanks to the activities of visitor centers, by managing bodies and municipalities, including itineraries and excursions of a sporting, naturalistic, eno-gastronomic, historical-artistic and religious nature.

Stretching across the territories of as many as 18 municipalities, the park flaunts many centers of tourist attraction, such as the sites of San Giovanni

Rotondo and San Marco in Lamis, the Swabian castle of Monte Sant'Angelo, the Manor of Manfredonia, and the coastal resorts of Peschici and Vieste.

Gargano National Park

SALINE OF MARGHERITA OF SAVOIA

Guardians of the "white gold," the Margherita di Savoia Salt Pans flaunt a history spanning thousands of years amid jewels of industrial archaeology and the halls of the Historical Museum.

The Margherita di Savoia Salt Pans are situated on a plain of the Tavoliere delle Puglie overlooking the Adriatic Sea.

Consisting of a vast expanse of calm water divided into basins for the production of sea salt, it is the largest salt pan in Italy and one of the largest in the entire Mediterranean basin.

Lake Salpi was once located here: its salt deposits were used as far back as the Neolithic period and also by the Greeks and Romans. Man's interest stems from economic reasons but also for the therapeutic virtues of the Acque Madri, or red waters, used in spa treatments.

Over time the land use has undergone functional changes to new salt extraction techniques. Important testimonies of industrial archaeology, the structures built by Ferdinand I of Bourbon in the first half of the 19th century are still all to be discovered.

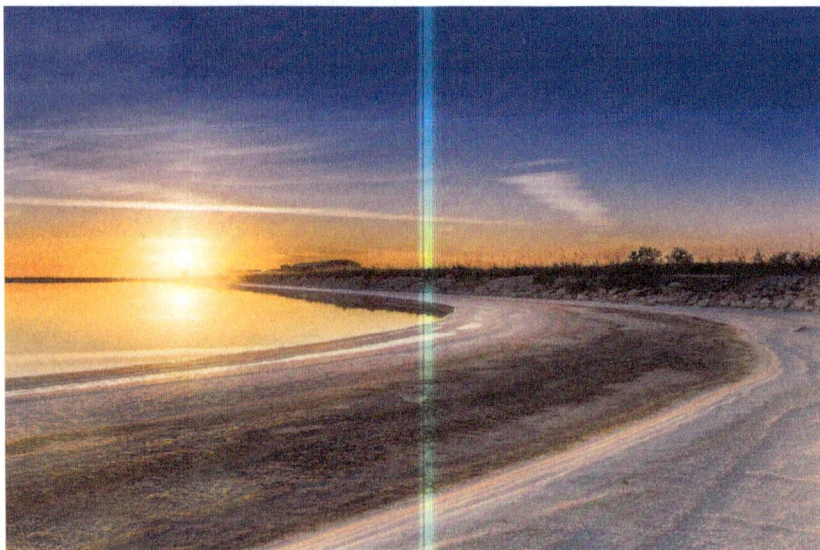

Saline of Margherita di Savoia

Worth visiting is the Historical Museum of the Salt Pans, housed in an old salt warehouse adjacent to the 16th-century Torre delle Saline.

The flora of the area is distinguished by its degree of specialization to withstand the high aridity rate such as saltcedar and cacti with fleshy leaves. From a wildlife point of view, the area represents a suitable habitat for a great variety and quantity of waterfowl such as herons, egrets, night herons, and tufted warblers.

ALTA MURGIA NATIONAL PARK

Custodian of the last example of Mediterranean steppe in Italy, the Alta Murgia National Park encompasses dry-stone buildings, fortified farms and the magic of Castel del Monte.

Stretching from the Adriatic coast to the Lucanian foothills, the Alta Murgia National Park guards the last example of Mediterranean steppe in Italy.

Consisting mainly of limestone rocks, tuffs and clay deposits, the entire plateau is rich in mushrooms, lampascioni, wild asparagus and cardoncelli.

Alta Murgia National Park

Standing out in the greenery are the dry-stone buildings that served as animal shelters during transhumance. Mighty and majestic farms, some fortified like real castles, were the vital centers of the local agricultural economy since the 15th century.

The pride and joy of the park is Castel del Monte, the mysterious manor built by "stupor mundi" Frederick II as a hunting lodge once enlivened by falconers and game.

In a succession of rock formations, dense forests and vast steppe expanses, the Alta Murgia National Park flaunts barren pastures where mosses and lichens sprout while the undergrowth is rich in wild orchids and dog roses. There are also numerous native animal species such as the cricket hawk, which has become a symbol of the park.

TORRE GUACETO MARINE PROTECTED AREA

Dominated by the centuries-old coastal lookout, the Torre Guaceto Marine Protected Area stretches with its cliffs and sandy shoreline along the Adriatic coast between Punta Penna Grossa and the rocks of Apani.

Located on the Adriatic coast of upper Salento, not far from Carovigno and San Vito dei Normanni, the Torre Guaceto Marine Protected Area stretches along an 8-kilometer stretch of coastline between Punta Penna Grossa and the Apani rocks.

The landscape of the reserve is characterized by coastal dunes, with some stretches of gray dunes approaching 15 meters in height.

In the Torre Guaceto Reserve, Posidonia oceanica meadows represent one of the most characteristic habitats of the sandy seabed between 3 and 25 meters deep. In the blue, among the brown and red algae and sea lettuce, limpets, sea tomatoes, sea sponges and anemones find refuge. Noteworthy is the Pinna Nobilis, a large bivalve mollusk at risk of extinction.

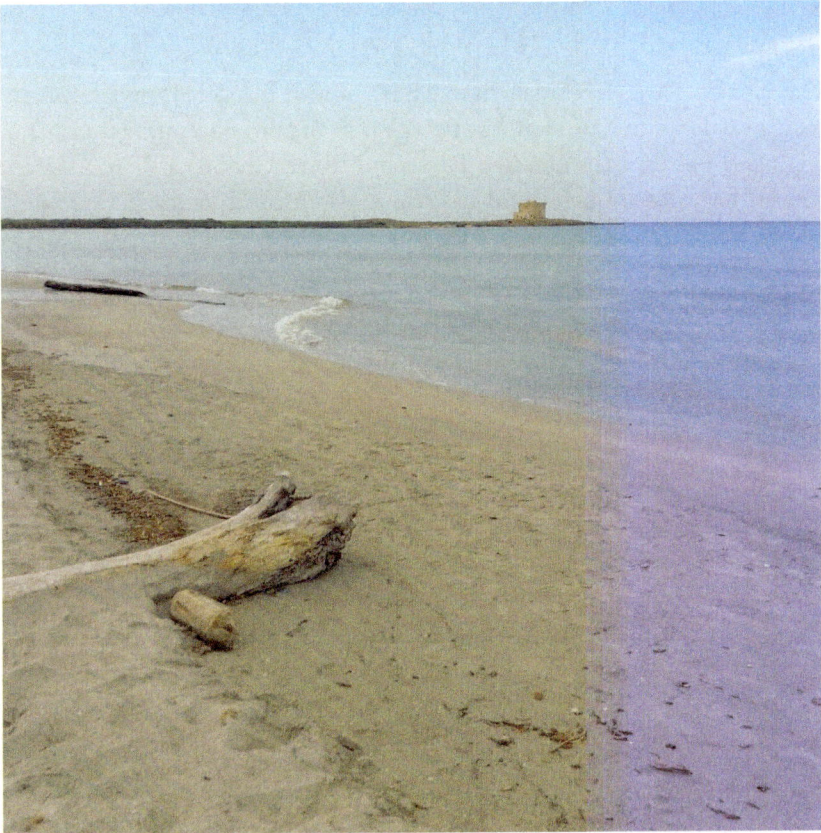

Torre Guaceto

CHIDRO RIVER NATURE RESERVE

The Chidro River is a small river whose mouth is located on the Ionian coast of Salento in San Pietro in Bevagna, in the province of Taranto, and originates between the Borraco River and Torre Colimena. It is a watercourse that runs underground for about 10 km until it reaches a spring known as a "crater" that is immersed in a nature reserve.

From there the river of water runs for a stretch of 500 meters and reaches the sea, near San Pietro in Bevagna beach and before flowing into the sea it forms three small lakes. The mouth of the Chidro River, then, flows into the waters of the Ionian Sea, and is an ideal place for torrid summer days thanks to its clear, cool water.

The surrounding setting made up of green vegetation around the river emphasizes a contrast of colors and creates a breathtaking scenery along with the brilliant waters of the river. It is also interesting to know that, not far from the mouth, valuable sarcophagi from the Roman era lie on the seabed in front of it. In addition, the river is frequented by many diving enthusiasts, curious to explore this underwater place rich in underwater beauty.

Chidro River Nature Reserve

The legend of St. Peter the Apostle circulates about this river, in which it is said that the Apostle crossed the river weeping, and that tears shed turned into shells. The custom desired by the ancient inhabitants of the area to collect the shells was precisely to remember him and keep the petrified tears as relics of the Apostle.

The temperature of the river water is between 18-20 degrees and the health benefits it confers are indeed many, from hydrotherapy, the cold river water also helps to improve blood circulation, regulate temperature and regenerate the body, useful for relieving depression, improving breathing and maintaining healthy skin and hair. Therefore, an ideal place to feel healthier and happier.

MERCADANTE FOREST

The Mercadante forest, which was created about 30 km from Bari to stem the floods that struck the Apulian capital in the early 20th century, is a vast green area of about 1,300 hectares that starts from nearby Cassano delle Murge and reaches (in a small part) the outskirts of Altamura.

Like all forests, Mercadante's offers visitors an evocative landscape rich in vegetation: from pines to holm oaks, from cypresses to oaks to eucalyptus trees and much, much more.

Of course, there is no shortage of different species of birds, reptiles and mammals that complement all the beauty of what has been dubbed Bari's green lung.

Immersing oneself in the Mercadante Forest means being able to enjoy the fantastic paths and trails characteristic of the forest, which, let us remind you, are equipped with restaurants, bike areas (several tourists organize bike excursions) and above all picnic areas (they certainly could not be missed) complete with wooden tables and benches to enjoy a snack in the heart of nature.

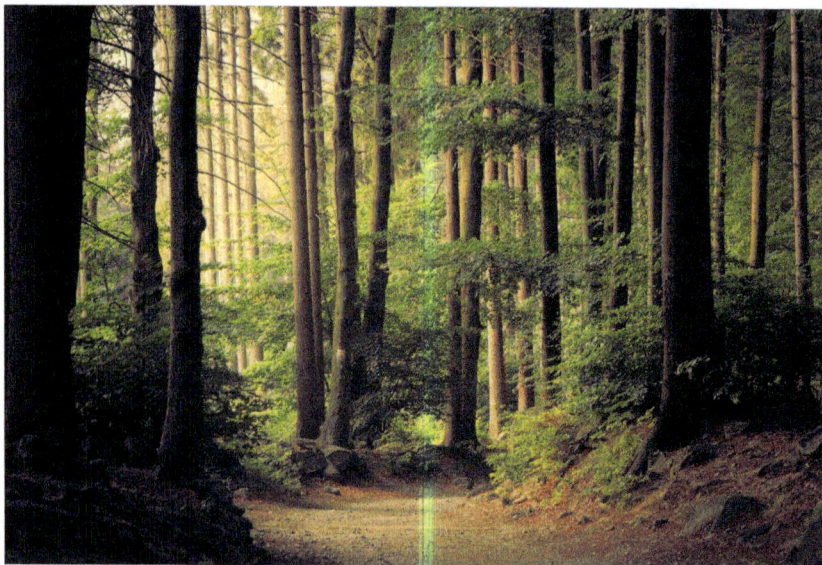

Mercadante Forest

There is also clearly no shortage of toilets and play areas for children, ideal for families.

This beautiful place around Bari undoubtedly deserves your attention, especially if you want to escape from the typical chaos of the big city or simply if you are a lover of relaxation, nature and animals.

Yes, because in addition to the classic reptiles and mammals of the vegetation, during walks in the Mercadante Forest you might also encounter different types of animals such as horses, deer, donkeys, foxes, fawns and others, all of course cared for and protected by the forest ranger.

So, as you can imagine, the Mercadante forest will definitely enter your notebook of notes, precisely among the most beautiful places to see around the Apulian capital.

A real gem to visit especially, or preferably, between spring and summer, to best experience every corner of this beautiful green lung, the relaxation areas and all the sweetness of the animals that the forest has been guarding for so many years.

Entrance to the Mercadante Forest is of course free, which is why everyone's responsibility is needed to continue to preserve it in that of the Alta Murgia National Park.

CASTELLANA CAVES

Rightly called the "Wonder of Puglia," the Castellana Caves are a complex of underground cavities of karst origin located in the municipality of Castellana Grotte, in the southeastern Murge region of Puglia.

The corridors, tunnels and caves wind for a length of 3348 meters at a depth of about 70 meters, descending to a maximum of 122 meters from the surface.

To visit the Castellana Caves is to have a unique experience. In an amazing scenery, one crosses caves with fantastic names, canyons and deep chasms, discovers fossils, stalactites, stalagmites, concretions with incredible shapes and unexpected colors. It is an amazing tour that transports the visitor to a wonderful world whose history dates back as much as ninety to one hundred million years.

Among the others, two are the most surprising caves. The first, the one from which the tourist trail begins, is the Grave. A large cave, it is distinguished by an opening at the top to connect the underground world with the outside world. The swallowhole, created in a natural way, lets light filter inside the Cave realizing extraordinary plays of light.

Another cavern leaves everyone breathless: the White Cave. Elegant and majestic, it fascinates with the richness and whiteness of the alabaster. A truly unmissable spectacle.

Castellana Caves

CAVES OF POLIGNANO

Polignano is well known, and not only in Italy, for its enchanting scenic beauty. A crystal-clear sea bathes its coasts in overlapping layers, like "a book impetrated by time," and laps and foams in the numerous caves, which, from north to south, open in the cliffs.

From the sea, the whole conformation of the coast can be grasped, dotted with ravines and caves, stone squiggles that rise above the water and preserve in their alvei wonders of vastness and depth of proportions as well as richness of colors, mingled by the shades of limestone slapped by mistral storms, the thudding of sea waves and darts of light, which from the universe precipitate sghimbly and bounce between stones and water.

Polignano's caves, the majority of which are surveyed by the Catasto speleo-logico, deserve to be visited to enjoy the phantasmagorical plays of light, which glimmer inside, the result of refraction between a shining sky and a clear sea, and to admire the portentous work of burin, which nature, using water and wind, has been able to accomplish over the centuries. An enjoy-ment that needs time. In a week's time it is possible to get enthusiastic about this gruyère of the earth, which smells salty and sounds, according to the uzzolo of the winds, the suavity of bonacce and the harshness of storms.

The caves can be reached by swimming or in chartered boats.

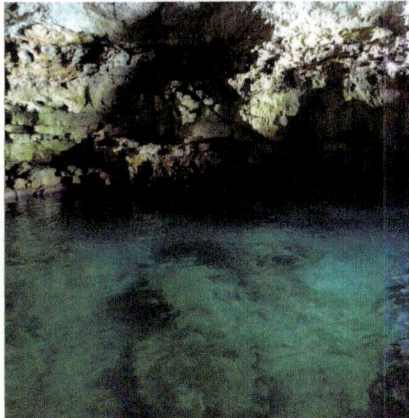

Caves of Polignano

ITRIA VALLEY

Itria Valley is an area in the heart of Puglia between the provinces of Bari, Brindisi and Taranto also known as Murgia dei Trulli, in the southern part of the Murge and north of Alto Salento.

It is still an authentic land of ancient traditions and with a strong connection to the natural environment, which is reflected in the local food and wine: expanses of olive trees as far as the eye can see, almond trees, vineyards and orchards, among which sprout the many farmhouses, many of which are still inhabited and often converted back into tourism-related activities and facilities.

And then the trulli, those dwellings so particular and characteristic of the Itria Valley, which locally are called casedde: there are about 15,000 of them scattered among the whitewashed towns of this area, so full of treasures of art and culture.

Where does the name "Itria Valley" come from? Probably from the chapel of Our Lady of Odegitria located in the Church of the Capuchins in Martina Franca, where an ancient effigy bears witness to the cult of Byzantine origin introduced in the early 1000s by Basilian monks.

The valley was called, in fact, "of the Madonna of the Odegitria," but over time the toponym was synthesized into Valle d'Itria, and the Madonna who leads the way is located precisely at a crossroads where the passage of history is felt.

Itria Valley

CHAPTER 5

AREAS OF HISTORICAL AND CULTURAL INTEREST TO SEE

CASTEL OF MONTE

A symbol of harmonious blending of cultural elements from northern Europe, the Muslim world and classical antiquity, Castel del Monte, a unique masterpiece of medieval architecture, has been on the UNESCO World Heritage List since 1996.

The castle, dating back to the 13th century (the earliest document available to us for dating it is 1240), was commissioned by Frederick II of Swabia, ruler of the Holy Roman Empire.

While the structure appears peripheral today, at the time of its construction it stood not far from the axis that connected the two important settlements of Andria and Garagnone, near Gravina. It's very location made the castle an essential element in the communication system within the network Frederick II wanted.

For a long time, it's intended use was debated: the term castrum, in fact, refers directly to a defensive function, but the presence of some "accessory" structures and the refinement of the sculptural repertoire have led to the hypothesis that it was also residential and representative.

Built directly on a rocky bank, the castle is known for its octagonal shape. On each of the corners are grafted eight towers made of local limestone.

The courtyard, also octagonal in shape, is characterized, like the entire building, by the color contrast achieved through the use of coral breccia, limestone, and marble. At one time there were also rich sculptural furnishings, of which only a slab depicting the Knights' Court and a fragment of an anthropomorphic figure remain to this day.

In the sixteen trapezoidal-shaped halls, eight on each floor, the keystones of the crosses are characteristic, each decorated with anthropomorphic, zoomorphic, and phytomorphic elements.

Some towers house cisterns for collecting rainwater, some of which is also conveyed to the cistern below the central courtyard. Others house bathrooms, equipped with a latrine and wash basin.

Castel del Monte

HISTORICAL CENTER OF BARI

The historic center of Bari more commonly called "Bari Vecchia" is a pleasant discovery for both tourists and locals living in other neighborhoods.

The old part of Bari is a labyrinth of narrow streets often underestimated and victims of past prejudices that today, however, are experiencing a strong cultural redemption not only because they are home to the relics of the world's most revered saint: St. Nicholas.

The richness of Bari's old town, the people who inhabit it and the scents in the air have made it possible to erase from memory the fear that old Bari was dangerous, revaluing the oldest part of the Apulian capital as a hub of cultural and experiential activities for tourists and non-tourists alike. In addition to the many churches that Bari's historic center flaunts (first and foremost the basilica of St. Nicholas and the cathedral of San Sabino), the oldest part of Bari offers a wonderful medieval castle, the longest waterfront in Italy and lots and lots of good food.

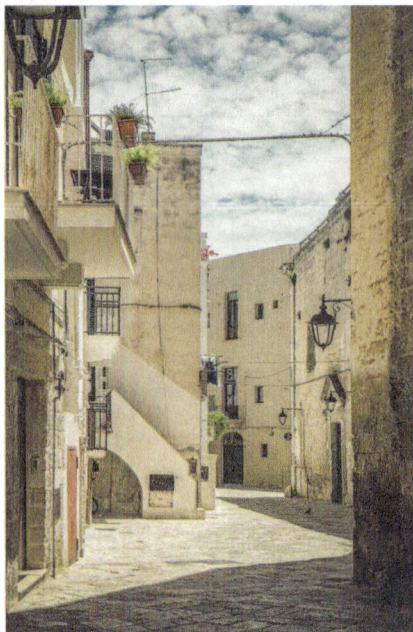

Center of Bary

BASILICA SAN NICOLA OF BARI

Old Bari is an important place of pilgrimage because it houses the relics of St. Nicholas in the Basilica dedicated to his figure revered throughout the world and is just one, perhaps the most important, of old Bari 25 wonderful churches.

The opening hours of the Basilica of St. Nicholas are continuous from 7 a.m. to 9 p.m., allowing visitors from all parts of the world to admire the ecumenical character of the Christian religion and possibly participate in two different cults: Christian Catholic and Greek Orthodox.

Before entering, it is advisable to stand in the center of the Square to admire its simple majesty, the Romanesque-Pugliese architecture, and the asymmetrical shape redesigned around 1100 on the remains of the Palace of Catalan (Greek-Byzantine governor of Southern Italy).

Inside, admission is free and you can discover so many stories related to the church and the icon of St. Nicholas, such as, for example, his life of charity lived around the year 300 AD as bishop of Myra - present-day Turkey, the translation of his relics stolen in 1087 by 62 sailors, his holy manna, the patronal feast dedicated to him.

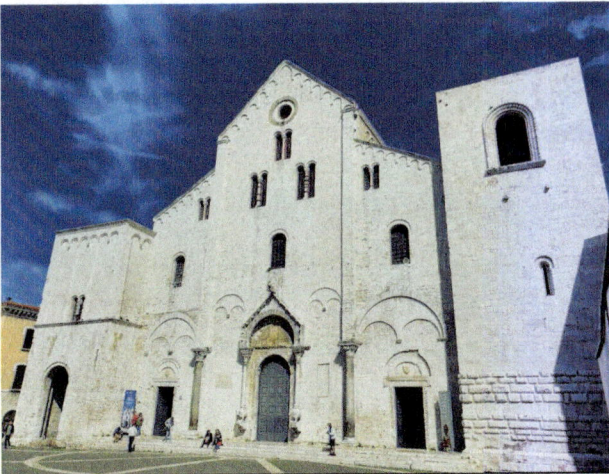

Basilica San Nicola of Bari

HISTORICAL CENTER OF LECCE

Lecce is a pearl of Baroque art and culture, fulcrum of the Salento area and cultural center of the entire province.

Its historic center, whose beauty is unanimously recognized internationally, is capable of enclosing enormous cultural and architectural heritages, in an incredible mixture of different styles and eras that have inevitably left their mark on the ancient city walls of the Salento capital. Any trip that includes even a one-day visit to Lecce cannot be separated from viewing the historic center.

A good starting point may be the Bourbon Obelisk located near Porta Napoli, one of the four historic city gates (the others being Porta Rudiae and Porta San Biagio, plus Porta San Martino, no longer extant). Entering through Porta Napoli offers an evocative feeling of complete immersion in the city's cultural heritage, entering for all intents and purposes the real old city. The gate, built by Charles V in the 16th century and recently restored, was intended to represent the grandeur of the kingdom, and to this day it succeeds very well in conveying such feelings to all who pass through it.

Immediately after the gate (the historic center is pedestrian-only, completely closed to traffic) you take the charming cobbled Via Palmieri, on the route of which you can admire the historic Paisiello Theater and at the end of which you suddenly come to Piazza Duomo. The Piazza, one of the most beautiful in the entire city, is nothing more than a large courtyard, which provides a wonderful backdrop to the Cathedral of Lecce (which is definitely worth a visit) and is colored with incredible bright red hues at sunset, or spectacular plays of light at nightfall.

Going then along Via Vittorio Emanuele II it is possible to admire an innumerable series of alleys and courtyards, until you find on the street the church of Sant'Irene, recently renovated and absolutely worth visiting inside and admiring externally for its spectacular facade. Continuing on the same street we reach Piazza Sant'Oronzo, the true hub and central pivot of the city. In the center is the She-wolf, the city's symbol par excellence, while to the side you can admire the Sedile, with its spectacular stained-glass entrance window, and the Roman amphitheater, often the scene of performances and cultural events. Near the square also it is impossible not to visit the Basilica of Santa Croce and the Palazzo dei Celestini, true jewels of the city and universally recognized as world masterpieces of Baroque art.

Historical Center of Lecce

ALBEROBELLO AND ITS TRULLI

Trulli, typical limestone dwellings in Alberobello in southern Apulia, are outstanding examples of dry-stone slab construction, a technique dating back to prehistoric times and still used in this region. Although rural trulli are scattered throughout the Itria Valley, the highest concentration of the best-preserved examples of this architectural form can be found in the town of Alberobello, with more than 1,500 structures in the districts of Monti and Aja Piccola.

Trulli are traditional dry-stone huts with roofs composed of slabs set in dry-stone. Trulli generally served as temporary shelters or as permanent homes by small landowners or agricultural workers. Trulli were built of roughly worked limestone, quarried during excavations for underground cisterns, stones collected from the countryside and from surrounding rocky outcrops. Such buildings have the characteristic rectangular structure with a conical roof made of embedded stones.

The whitewashed walls of the trulli are built directly on the limestone foundations and constructed using the dry-stone masonry technique, without mortar or cement. A doorway and small windows open on the double-clad walls with an incoherent core. An interior hearth and alcoves are set in the thick walls. The roofs are also double-layered: an inner vaulted covering of cone-shaped stones, culminating in keystones, and an impermeable outer cone consisting of limestone slabs, known as chianche or chiancarelle. The roofs of the buildings often bear white ash inscriptions of mythological or religious significance, and end with a decorative pinnacle that was intended to ward off evil influences or bad luck.

Water is collected through eaves protruding from the base of the roof, from which it then flows through a gutter to a cistern below the dwelling. About a thousand years ago (1,000 B.C.), the area of present-day Alberobello was sprinkled with rural settlements. The settlements grew to form the present districts of Aia Piccola and Monti. By the mid-16th century, the Monti district was occupied by some 40 trulli, but it was not until 1620 that the settlement began its expansion.

In 1797, toward the end of feudal rule, the name Alberobello was adopted, and Ferdinand IV of Bourbon, king of Naples, gave the locality the title of royal city. After that period, the building of new trulli fell into decline.

Between 1909 and 1936, parts of Alberobello were designated as protected monuments of cultural heritage.

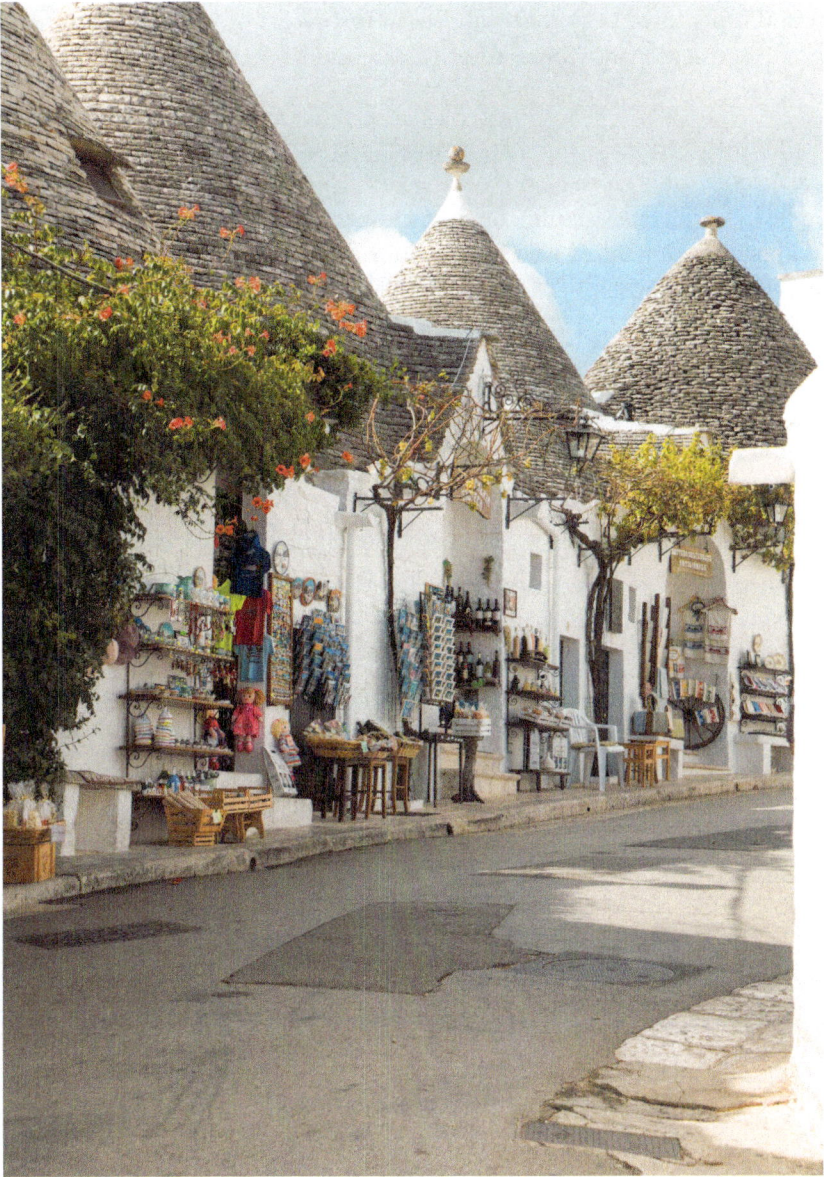

Alberobello and its Trulli

OSTUNI: THE WHITE CITY

Called the "White City" because of the entirely lime-covered dwellings found in its town center, Ostuni is a tourist resort of great value that has been awarded many times for the exceptional natural integrity of its beaches.

The historic center is full of wonders to see, including religious and civic architecture of great value such as the Church of San Vito Martire, the Co-cathedral and the Column of Sant'Oronzo, which we recommend you admire via an organized walking tour, during which a local guide will reveal secrets and curiosities.

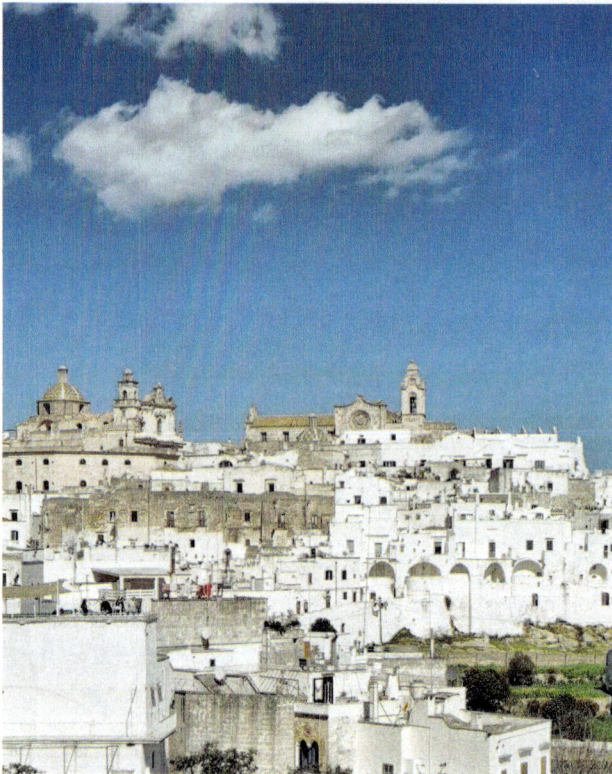

Ostuni

MOUNT SANT'ANGELO

Monte Sant'Angelo is known all over the world for its religious history, becoming a must-see destination in Michaelic pilgrimages. Saints, emperors, popes, kings or simple faithful have come here to kneel before the altar of Archangel Michael.

The town is the highest in the Gargano (843 m.) and is situated in an admirable panoramic position on a spur south of the promontory, with breathtaking views open to the west over the Tavoliere and to the south over the Gulf of Manfredonia.

Home to the Gargano National Park and a UNESCO World Heritage Site, the town's life is centered around the Sanctuary of St. Michael the Archangel, built between the 5th-6th centuries when, according to tradition, apparitions of the archangel occurred in a cave. The Lombards, who ruled in southern Italy at that time, made it their national shrine. It quickly became a renowned center throughout Christendom and a must-see destination, not only for pilgrims from all over Europe, but also for Crusaders leaving for Jerusalem.

The town has an elongated shape around the axis formed by Via Manfredi; this reconnects on the western side of the town to the state road toward San Giovanni Rotondo and on the eastern side to a branch of the Garganica state road.

Mount Sant'Angelo

CHAPTER 6

HOW TO ARRIVE IN APULIA

Apulia is easily accessible using the highway and railway networks. It is also possible to get to Puglia by air from several Italian cities and major European capitals. Finally, thanks to its three ports, there is also a sea option to reach Puglia by ship or ferry.

BY PLANE

There are two main airports in Puglia: Karol Wojtyla Airport in Bari and Salento Airport in Brindisi. Both airports are well connected to major Italian and European cities through direct flights or with stopovers in Milan and Rome.

• Bari Airport is the main airport in Puglia. It is located in Palese, 9 km from Bari; consequently, it is possible to reach the city center by train, by bus with the AMTAB service line 16, or by using the shuttle service operated by Autoservice Tempesta. In addition, Puglia Air Bus connects the airport to several cities, including Matera.

• Brindisi Airport is about 6 km from the city center and about 35 km from Lecce; therefore, it is the best option for reaching Salento by air. The transportation company STP Brindisi connects the airport to the city and marina of Brindisi, as well as to the city of Lecce. In addition, Puglia Air Bus connects the airport to several cities, including Matera.

BY TRAIN

The State Railways serve the entire region quite well, thus making the train an excellent option for getting to and around Puglia. The Adriatic railway line connects Bologna to both Lecce and Taranto, with planned stops in Foggia and Bari. In contrast, the line connecting Rome to Taranto stops in Naples and Bari.

More information can be found on the official website of Ferrovie dello Stato www.trenitalia.com.

The main railway stations in Apulia are Foggia, Bari, Brindisi, Lecce and Taranto, all of which are easily accessible and located near the city center. There are also regional companies that offer regular services in the six provinces. The main domestic lines are:

•Taranto - Ginosa (in the direction of Reggio Calabria)

•Barletta - Spinazzola

•Spinazzola - Gioia del Colle

•Foggia - Manfredonia

•Cervaro - Rocchetta S. Antonio – Lacedonia

BY BUS

Traveling by bus could be a viable and cheaper alternative to the train, as well as a fantastic opportunity to cross several places in one trip.

Buses normally stop in even the smallest towns, and local companies offer regular runs to and within Puglia. For more information on services, costs, and schedules, we recommend visiting the websites of the different companies:

•Marozzi: www.marozzivt.it rides to/from Naples, Rome, Florence, Pisa and Siena.

•Marino bus: www.marinobus.it runs to/from milan, verona, vicenza, florence, siena, livorno

and empoli.

•Miccolis: www.miccolis-spa.it rides to/from Potenza, Salerno and Naples.

•Scoppio: www.autolineescoppio.it rides to/from Catania e Palermo.

•Lentini autolinee: lentini.autolinee.it runs to/from livorno, la spezia, genova and savona.

BY BOAT/FERRY

Puglia boasts several ports along the coast. However, only the ports of Bari and Brindisi are also used for tourist connections.

The Port of Bari offers daily connections to Durres in Albania, Antivari in Montenegro, Corfu, Igoumenitsa, and Patras in Greece.

The Port of Brindisi offers daily connections to Vlora in Albania, Corfu, Igoumenitsa, Kefalonia, Paxos, Zakynthos, and Patras in Greece, and also to Çeşme in Turkey.

The Port of Taranto is one of the most important ports in Italy and the entire Mediterranean in the military and industrial fields. It is also connected to the Middle East and China, mainly for commercial purposes.

HOW GET TO LECCE

A direct bus provides transportation from Bari and Brindisi airports to Lecce. The bus stop in Lecce, the Lecce City Terminal, is located at the northern entrance to the city, not far from the historic center. Depending on the location of your accommodation in Lecce, you can get around on foot or by bus. Line 21 "Navetta Foro Boario" is a shuttle service that connects the large parking lot near City Terminal with the castle, not far from Piazza Sant'Oronzo.

City Terminal offices close at 5:30 p.m.; the staff could certainly provide you with additional information to help you get to your accommodation.

If you arrive at Bari Airport, it is possible to reach Lecce by train once you arrive at Bari Centrale train station. In addition to being connected to major Italian cities (info on Trenitalia.com), Lecce is also served by a local network, that of Ferrovie Sud Est (FSE), which connects the Salento capital to Gallipoli and Otranto, but also to some towns in the Itria Valley, such as Martina Franca, Alberobello, Locorotondo and Cisternino. Inside the Lecce Station you can find the appropriate FSE ticket office. STP buses leave from the square in front of the station. At the station bar you can buy both bus and regional train tickets.

HOW GET TO MATERA FROM BARI

- Direct bus connection - From Bari Airport to Matera: see Pugliairbus about 75 min.
- Train + Train: 1. From Bari Airport to Bari Centrale train station. There are trains every 30 min connecting the airport to Bari Centrale station (about 15 min.); once in Bari Centrale, you can reach Matera by train. See Ferrovie Appulo Lucane about 90 min.
- Shuttle Bus + Train: There is a shuttle bus from Bari Airport to Bari Centrale station by Autoservizi Tempesta (about 30 min, departures every hour); having arrived at Bari Centrale, it is possible to reach Matera by train with Ferrovie Appulo Lucane.

Printed in Great Britain
by Amazon